DAVID BAILEY

PETER BEARD

ILSE BING

BILL BURKE

WILLIAM CLAXTON

MICHEL COMTE

LYNN DAVIS

PATRICK DEMARCHELIER

ARTHUR ELGORT

RALPH GIBSON

PAUL GRENDON

JAN GROOVER

EVELYN HOFER

DENNIS HOPPER

MARK KLETT

CHERYL KORALIK

ANNIE LEIBOVITZ

PETER LINDBERG

MARCIA LIPPMAN

MARY ELLEN MARK

KURT MARKUS

STEVEN MEISEL

SUSAN MEISELAS

SHEILA METZNER

HERB RITTS

PAOLO ROVERSI

SEBASTIÃO SALGADO

ALDO SESSA

BERT STERN

PHIL STERN

JUDITH TURNER

MAX VADUKUL

JAVIER VALLHONRAT

ALBERT WATSON

BRUCE WEBER

PICTURES

OF **PEACE**

Conceived and edited by Kim Zorn Caputo
Introduction by Grace Paley
Foreword by Roland Algrant
Designed by Sam Shahid

Alfred A. Knopf   New York 1991

THIS IS A BORZOI BOOK
PUBLISHED BY ALFRED A. KNOPF, INC.

Copyright © 1991 by Pictures of Peace, Inc.

All rights reserved under International and Pan-American Copyright Conventions.
Published in the United States by Alfred A. Knopf, Inc., New York, and
simultaneously in Canada by Random House of Canada Limited, Toronto.
Distributed by Random House, Inc., New York.

ISBN 0-679-40595-X
LC 91-52856

Manufactured in the United States of America

First Edition

In Memory of Henfil

PREFACE KIM ZORN CAPUTO

We were in Metropolitan Hospital; Henfil knew something horrible was happening to him. He said, "They're killing me. Look…all these dead bodies…Kim," he wet his lips, "you have to get me out of here." I did. We escaped the hospital where he had contracted AIDS through a blood transfusion. Three years later he died.

Henfil, Henrique de Sousa Filho, devoted his life to human rights. Everyone knew him in Brazil. I knew him in New York. He wrote, drew, and made movies that depicted the savagery, absurdity, and sadness of a world at unrest.

When I met him, my head full of the late sixties, I felt helpless in the face of his heroism. But he said, assuredly, "One day you will find your way." One and a half years ago I woke from a powerful dream. I heard his voice. This project began.

When I first began this, the dream of peace was not so remote as it is now. The end of the cold war filled us with hope. Eastern Europe was liberated from communism, soon to face the problems of Western capitalism. The time seemed ripe for a reassessment of our global concerns: human rights, housing, health care, unemployment, education.

Then, as we watched the troops depart for the Gulf, fathers, mothers, sons and daughters, drifting away from their homes to become soldiers, our hearts were breaking for families on both sides; going to fight and die for reasons beyond our comprehension. For peace is something we have already, like a summer bulb buried deep in the winter ground.

Peace is not only the absence of war. It is an atmosphere in which we have shelter enough to eat, and can move about and express ourselves freely.

As co-owner of a prominent New York photo lab, Lexington Labs, I was able to make my dream happen. For years, I have been working with the world's most exciting photographers, agencies, and publications. I have always wanted to bring them together for a worthy human rights event.

I asked the photographers whose work appears in this book to visualize the world at peace —to remember their dreams. Some of them bellowed, some paused and remembered quiet times, some of them chose to remind us of injustices.

Pictures of Peace began a world tour exhibition on April 3, 1991, at the Museum of Modern Art, Rio de Janeiro. As it travels through South America, the United States, Europe, Australia, and South Africa, the message is implicit.

All profits from this book, and related events, will be donated to Human Rights Watch.

We spend our lives unfolding mysteries,
brandishing our small discoveries
at the great unknown; marching with our friends
against loneliness; regaling
our ideas in pictures and song; singing
if all were well, if all were fair, if
all were free, I could be me.

The love of photography is the love of free expression.

Kim Zorn Caputo

FOREWORD ROLAND ALGRANT

Back in 1948, in the early part of its existence, the United Nations "adopted and proclaimed" one of the most important documents of this century—"The Universal Declaration of Human Rights."

Those who have read it already know that it is an amazingly simple, forthright, and beautiful piece of writing—even though, in its English translation, a good many of the phrases might seem awkward. Three of its articles, 5, 9, and 19, in many ways sum it up. These articles state that "no one shall be subjected to torture or to cruel, inhuman or degrading treatment or punishment," and that "no one shall be subjected to arbitrary arrest, detention or exile" and that "everyone has the right to freedom of opinion and expression."

If all the countries that participated in drafting this declaration had truly believed in it and abided by its thirty articles, there would be peace in the world today, and the wishes of the talented artists in this book would be fulfilled. But the reality is that most countries in the world do not pay much attention to this declaration despite having signed it. So we live in a world in which some forty countries are at war (civil or otherwise) and nearly fifteen million refugees need help—a world in which the issue of human rights is conveniently raised by governments only to make political points. It was left to private groups to impartially oversee human rights.

Human Rights Watch is a United States organization, formed in 1979, that monitors and reports on human rights violations in over sixty countries. As one of the two largest and most influential human rights organizations in the world today (the other being Amnesty International, based in London), Human Rights Watch publishes several books and dozens of news releases and reports throughout the year, which are widely quoted by the media and used by congressional committees. It is composed of six separate watch groups: Africa Watch, Americas Watch, Asia Watch, Helsinki Watch (so called for the 1975 accords signed by thirty-five governments in Eastern and Western Europe, the United States, and Canada), Middle East Watch, and the Fund for Free Expression (which operates on a worldwide basis).

All of us who are affiliated with the Human Rights Watch are very grateful to Kim Zorn Caputo, who created this book, and to the photographers who have filled it with their work and their thoughts.

Roland Algrant, Chairman,
Fund for Free Expression, Human Rights Watch

INTRODUCTION GRACE PALEY

Questions

A picture of peace, what is that? Is it a peaceful-looking picture, or any photograph taken during the absence of war? Is it that we need to give peace a good name? Why do we have to? Isn't it always better to be not killing others or mutilating them? Are there perfectly good reasons not to be living in peace? When we say "peace," do we mean the absence of all conflict, nonviolent struggles which are often quite fierce? Do we mean no pushing in the playground, no throwing sand in the sandbox? Do we mean peace except for "Oh well, boys will be boys"?

Do we think war is more exciting? Well, hasn't it been made to appear the most interesting moment in the bonding of men? Aren't there novels and autobiographies by men who've been to war that tell the young how interesting and exciting and important it was to have been at some particular battle, even though many of those men say they are now opposed to all war?

Haven't we lived through one of the strangest years in our lives and our country's coinciding life? Isn't it true that in the winter of '90–'91 a great many Americans (a majority of them women) were opposed to going to war and hoped for initiatives for alternative peaceful actions? Wasn't the feeling somewhat pacific even in Congress, which also hated the possibility of losing absolutely all its power to the determined President? Was this really because of the Vietnam Syndrome? Was this particular syndrome a collection of symptoms, like the questioning of authority? Did it also include a preference for mutual consideration and fear of the military and war in general? As syndromes go, wasn't that a good one?

Was it the day the President decided to go to war or a couple of days later that yellow ribbons appeared on trees and doorways and people? Did those ribbons really mean we had suddenly accepted authority? Can it be that overnight the country was wild for war, eager to censor disagreement? Is it true this included an eagerness to *be* censored? What does this all mean? What is its sorrowful meaning? How long before we take our syndrome back?

When I was asked to write an introduction for this book, *Pictures of Peace,* this large, hopeful international project, I remembered that many years ago, twenty-nine to be exact, our small neighborhood peace group, the Greenwich Village Peace Center, organized an event called Pictures of Peace. Since I think it worthwhile to tell a little history on

the way to the future, this is what happened there. Schoolchildren in the public, parochial, and private schools in the neighborhood were asked to draw an idea of their own peaceful world. There would be no winners. We had actually planned at first to suggest competitive possibility, but one of the elementary school teachers explained our own politics to us. Most of us, though we hadn't quite grasped it earlier, then understood it forever. So there would be an exhibition in one of the gyms, and finally Mrs. Kennedy and Mrs. Khrushchev would each be given a painting. These were graciously received at a poorly attended press conference.

What made us undertake this complicated project? We had been thinking mostly of the previous decade of deadly nuclear tests and arms buildups. But the nation Vietnam had just begun to sneak into our consciousness. At the same time, advisers, politicians, and generals were sneaking into the Vietnamese countryside and the back pages of our newspapers. We were more worried than usual.

The girls and boys who took part in our event were between six and fourteen years old. The war, which had barely begun in their childhood, would last another thirteen years for us and the suffering Vietnamese. Did those labored-over drawings and paintings, those talking, explaining mothers and teachers, the word "peace" said again and again— did any of that help a couple of youthful idealistic heads and hands against the recruiters and warmakers who had been waiting for years for those children to become the right size and age?

Modestly, we believe that neighborhood of attention had to have been useful. So, with this book in 1991, these Pictures of Peace, rare in our time, we add ourselves year by year, image by image, to the struggle for peaceful, just lives. We say, hold these pictures in your brainy heads. If you love this world, make use of them.

Grace Paley

"If the world were at peace, what would you shoot?"

DAVID BAILEY PICTURES OF PEACE

"'If the world were at peace,' I would carry on taking photographs
as I do now, and as I have done in the past."

Sudan, 1985
Catherine Bailey, 1985
Paloma Bailey, 1986

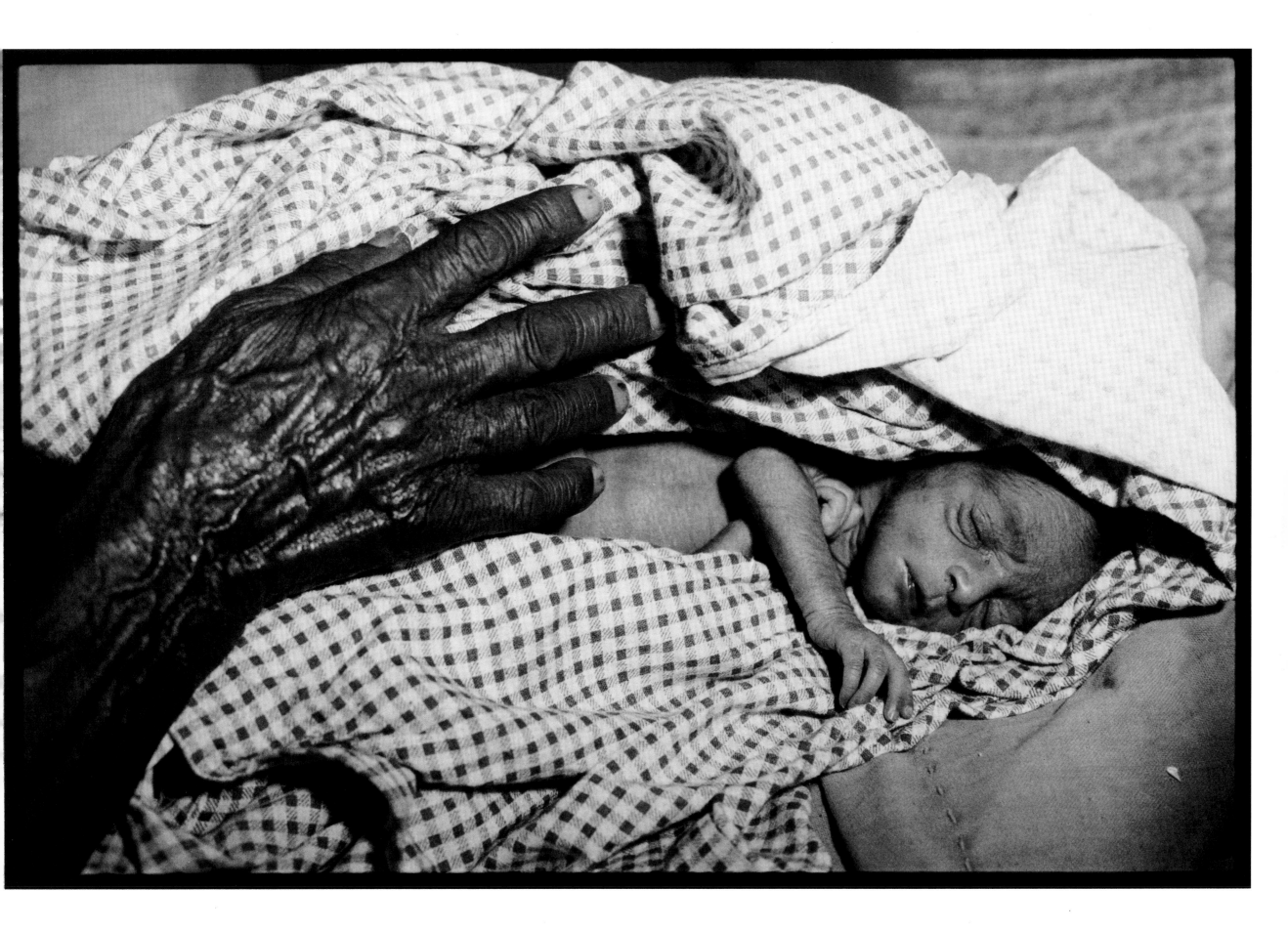

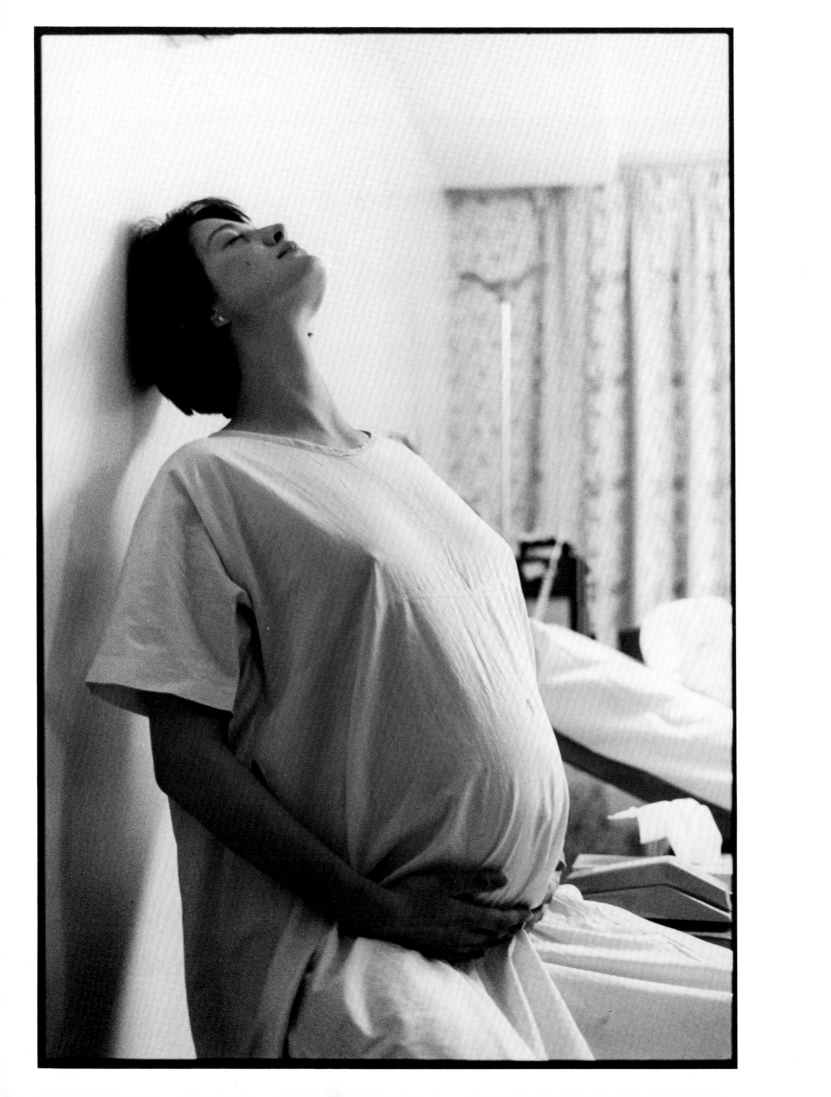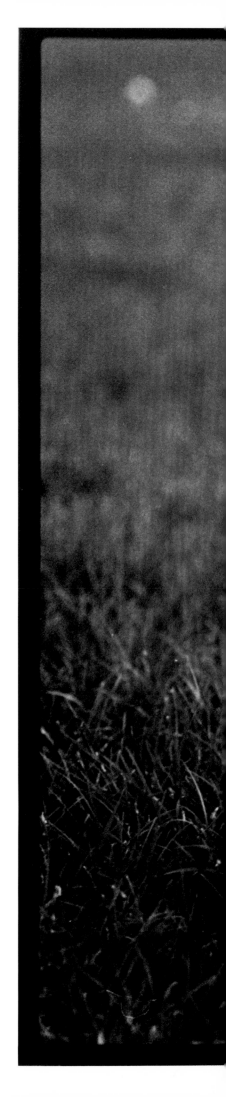

PETER BEARD PICTURES OF PEACE

Lake Rudolf, 1965–66, population dynamics survey, from *Eyelids of Morning*

A Last Stand of Elephants in Tsavo, a destroyed forest, 1971–72, from *End of the Game*

Tsavo National Park, before the die-off of 35,000 elephants, from *End of the Game*

Nor Dread Nor Hope Attend

Human beings finally achieved a population of one billion in about A.D. 1850...after three million years of evolution. Now, while in search of peace, we add a billion people every decade, despite mushrooming stress and density-related phenomena such as cancer, crime, heart disease, AIDS, drugs, pollution, violence, and war. Global habitat *carrying capacity* is overwhelmed, overburdened, fully diseased. Like the Calhoun rat studies, fanatic animalistic territorial squabbles dominate the world scene. Untold thousands of square miles of *wild-deer-ness* are converted annually into cement and steel, a soaring *Defense* budget, "constructive disarmament," state-of-the-arts Patriot missiles computer-targeting other missiles with chemical and nuclear warheads. The art and culture of the country is seen in the sky: *Tornados, Tomcats, Cheetahs, Jaguars, Eagles, Falcons, Tigersharks, Hornets, Harriers, Hawks, Sparrows, Blackbirds, Condors, Sidewinders, Cobras, Foxbats, Bearcats, Apaches, Thunderchiefs, and Phantoms.* War machinery. It's all up there.

"Sometimes on a safari... in a moment of extreme tension, I have met the eyes of my native companions, and have felt that we were at a great distance from one another, and that they were wondering at my apprehension of our risk. It made me reflect that perhaps they were, in life itself, within their own element, such as we can never be, like fishes in deep water which for the life of them cannot understand our fear of drowning. This assurance, this art of swimming, they had, I thought, because they had preserved a knowledge that was lost to us by our first Parents; Africa, amongst the continents, will teach it to you: that God and the Devil are one..." from *Out of Africa* by Karen Blixen

"All the animals languish, filling the air with lamentations. The woods fall in ruin. The mountains are torn open in order to carry away the metals which are produced there — But how can I speak of anything more wicked than men who raise hymns of praise to Heaven for those who, with greater zeal, have injured their country and the human race."
Leonardo da Vinci from *THE PROPHECIES*

And down here? Video games, war games, violence toys, treadmills, Abdomenizers, aerobic interval training, TV, Trivial Pursuit, plenty of plastic and blue hair, and those preposterous fake nails.

In our primitive stage of evolution, we're children at play in camouflage suits in *The Heart of Darkness*, lobbing missiles onto other continents. The one with the most toys wins. New World Order. Peace when we're dead.

tayiana, son of Lenana, at his father's grave, a mugumu tree that grew from his stomach... march 7th 1911 *from "SHADOWS of DESTINY"*

"Surely it is obvious enough, if one looks at the whole world, that it is becoming daily better cultivated and more fully peopled ... all places are now accessible, all are well known ... cultivated fields and subdued forests, flocks and herds of cattle have expelled wild beasts; sandy deserts are sown; marshes are drained — where once were solitary cottages there are now large cities. No longer are distant islands dreaded; everywhere are houses and inhabitants. Our teeming population is the strongest evidence: our numbers are burdensome to the world which can hardly supply us from its natural elements; our wants grow more and more keen, and our complaints more bitter in all mouths, whilst nature fails in affording us her usual sustenance. In every deed, pestilence, and famine and wars, and earthquakes have to be regarded as a remedy for nations, as the means of pruning the luxuriance of the human race." Tertullian 337 A.D.

a last stand of elephants in Tsavo, a destroyed forest (5,300 square miles) before the big die-off 1971-'72 *from "the END of the GAME"* 1977

Tsavo Park, before the die-off of 35,000 elephants

from "The End of the Game"/Peter Beard

The ruined wood,
We used to know,
Won't cry for retribution —
The men who have destroyed it
Will accomplish its revenge.

ILSE BING PICTURES OF PEACE

''I hope the timelessness and calm I feel when I take a picture are translated into my work.''

Cherub, 1946
Ode to Joy, Beethoven's Ninth Symphony Autograph, 1933–48
Gold Lamé Evening Shoes, 1935

BILL BURKE PICTURES OF PEACE

"The memory of war is not going to be erased in our lifetime.

 Peace is a nominal thing. The war continues in our minds.

"You can see the ruins. You can see it in our faces."

Fiddlin' Bill Livers, 1976

WILLIAM CLAXTON PICTURES OF PEACE

"'If the world were at peace,' I would select the following pictures...
Black-humor author Terry Southern, releasing Peace on an unsuspecting world,
Ojai, California, 1968
"because sometimes the simplest of acts can be the most symbolic and effective";

Fourth of July parade in a small western town in America, 1961
"and this one because it sums up patriotism, innocence, corn—America";

Kaffee Fassett, London, 1965
"to remind people what war is really about: beautiful young people
coming home dead."

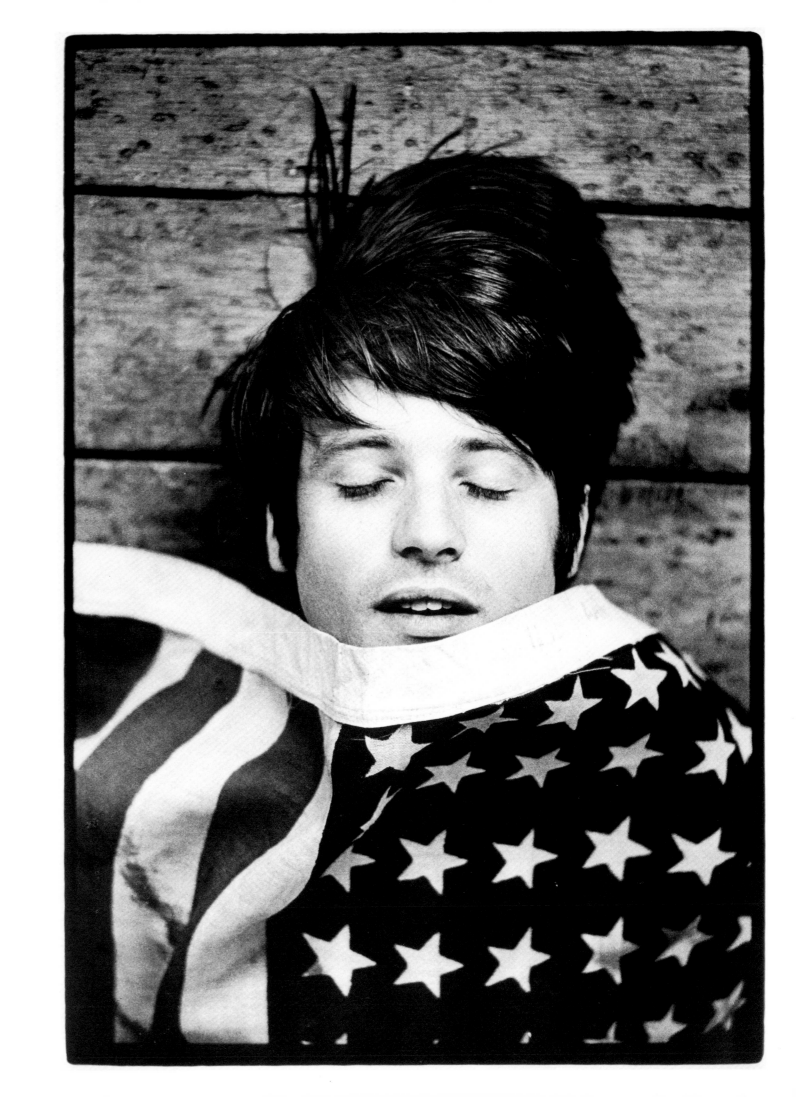

MICHEL COMTE PICTURES OF PEACE

"I had a dream and the dream goes on...."

Tyson (Dove), 1990
Tyson (Cross), Ohio, 1990

LYNN DAVIS PICTURES OF PEACE

"Light, water, ice, and clouds, constantly changing—the natural world,
transcendent and magical, dangerous and perfect, familiar and mysterious...."

1, 2, and 3, Untitled, Disco Bay, Greenland, 1988

PATRICK DEMARCHELIER PICTURES OF PEACE

''I love traveling. It's a habit. Two weeks in my New York studio, and the space is too
   small, so many deadlines...the phone never stops.

''My first priority is to relax my subjects. I want them to forget that they are being
   photographed. Madonna, or the Royal Family, no matter how different people look,
   photography has shown me that human beings act more or less the same way.

'''If the world were at peace,' my work would not change.''

Tibetan Man, 1988
Madonna/Silver, 1990

ARTHUR ELGORT PICTURES OF PEACE

"When I think about peace, I think about timelessness. Some things are inevitable—the rise and fall of the sun, birth, and ultimately death.

"Occasionally, as a photographer, one is able to capture that feeling of timelessness. It's a harmonious moment, where nothing else matters, resulting in an image of peace."

The Birth of Warren Arthur Elgort, December 6, 1989
Fourth of July, 1990, Martino House
Jardin des Tuileries, Paris, summer 1990

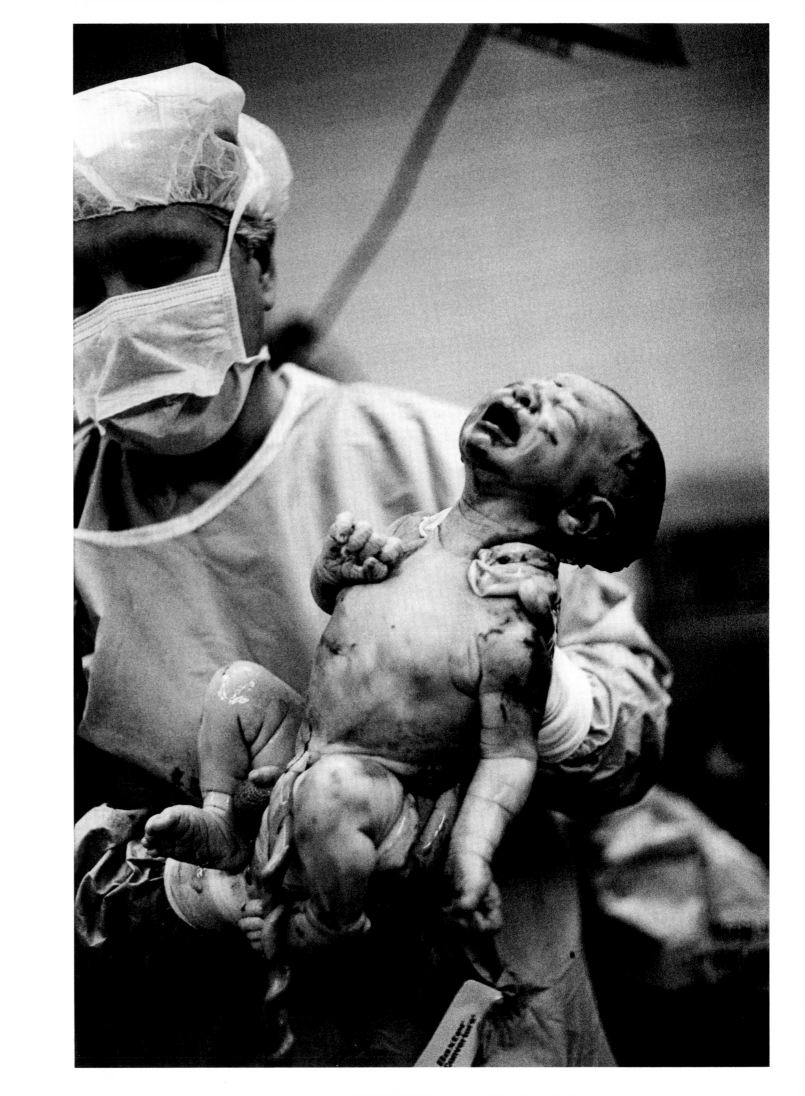

RALPH GIBSON PICTURES OF PEACE

"Peace is as much an inner spiritual state as it is a world condition. Perhaps for this
reason one can so determine that the first place to find peace is within oneself.

"The three images I have chosen reflect my personal attitudes toward love of
women, the pleasure of gazing out of a hotel-room window into a strange and
beautiful city, and the joy of feeding the body, as well as the soul."

Self-portrait, silhouette, Paris, 1983
Waiter with Silverware, Capri, 1983
Lips, Rome, 1987

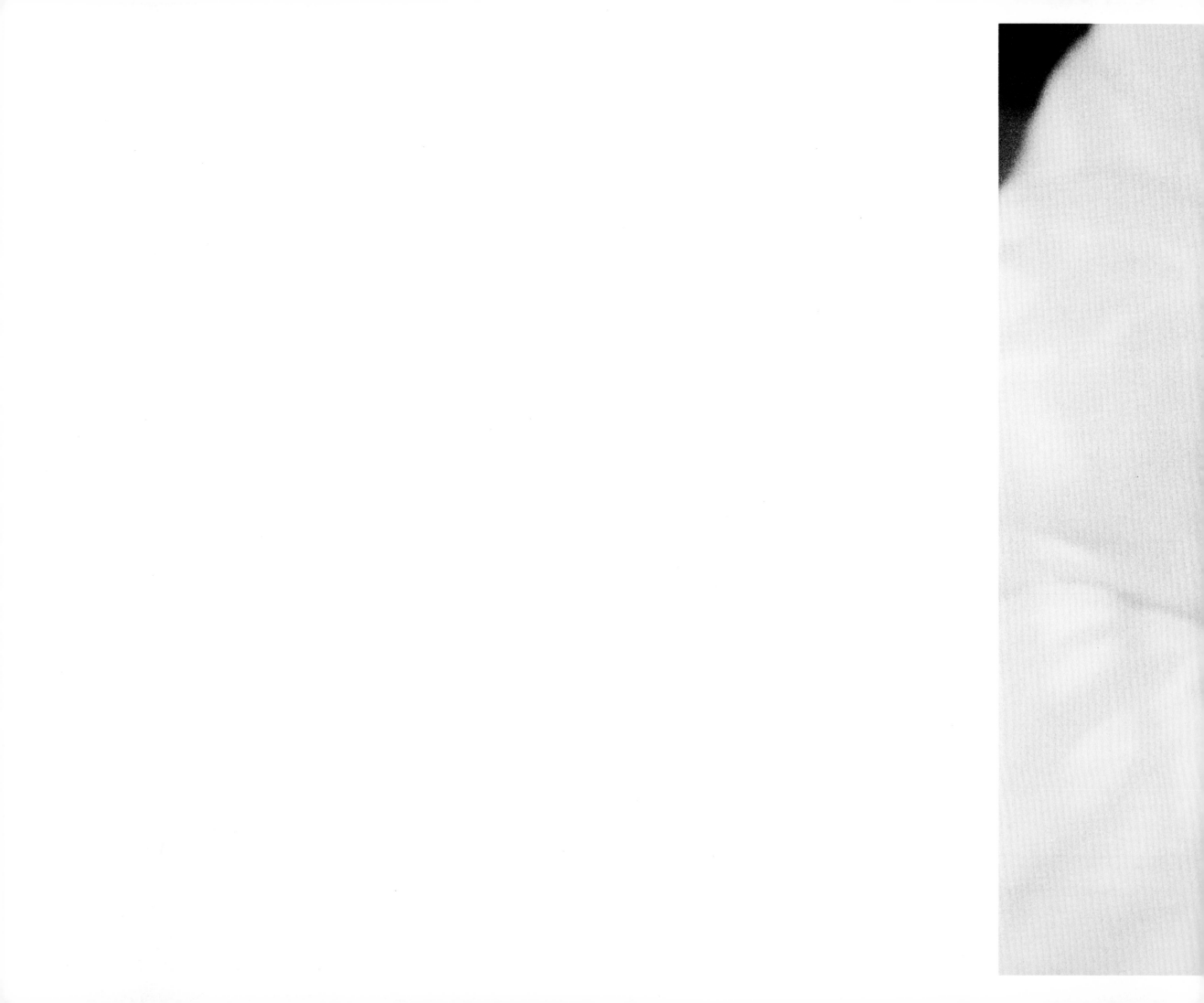

PAUL GRENDON PICTURES OF PEACE

"I would like to use a quote adopted by residents of Mier, a rural reserve in the northern Cape of South Africa, whose trust land is now under threat of sale through an act of parliament: 'If the one can live, all must be able to live.'"

Children Playing with (Homemade) Cart, Kammassies, Namaqualand, South Africa
Twee Rivier, Namaqualand, South Africa (Woman Cooling)
Winnowing Wheat, Steinkopf, Namaqualand, South Africa

JAN GROOVER PICTURES OF PEACE

311. 3 3/15 1986

305. 1 2/15 1986

EVELYN HOFER   PICTURES OF PEACE

"These images, the Duomo, the landscape, and the Italian family, detached
from the hurly-burly, stand still and reverent for the photographer. As
long as war does not physically destroy them, they remain as
monuments to the eternal."

Sheep near Huesca, Spain, 1963
The Duomo, Florence, 1987
An Italian Family, Bergamo, Italy, 1977

DENNIS HOPPER PICTURES OF PEACE

"What would I shoot if the world were at peace? I'd still be at war
with myself, so my images would be the same."

Selma, Alabama (March on Alabama), 1965
Biker Couple, 1962
Ron Davis, 1964

MARK KLETT PICTURES OF PEACE

"One of these pictures represents a landscape formerly under military control, a place that is now a public park. Ironically, the military presence saved this landscape from commercial development. The signs of former occupation have become decaying artifacts in a land that is reverting back to a natural state. This is a place full of hope. The other photograph is a reminder that time and history and human events belong to a continuous process. This is a relic of our ever-present and precarious relationship to the land, yet a tribute to our own impermanence."

Defense Icon, entrance to abandoned Nike radar installation on Wolf Ridge, California, 1987
Ventilated sedan east of Parker, Arizona, 1986

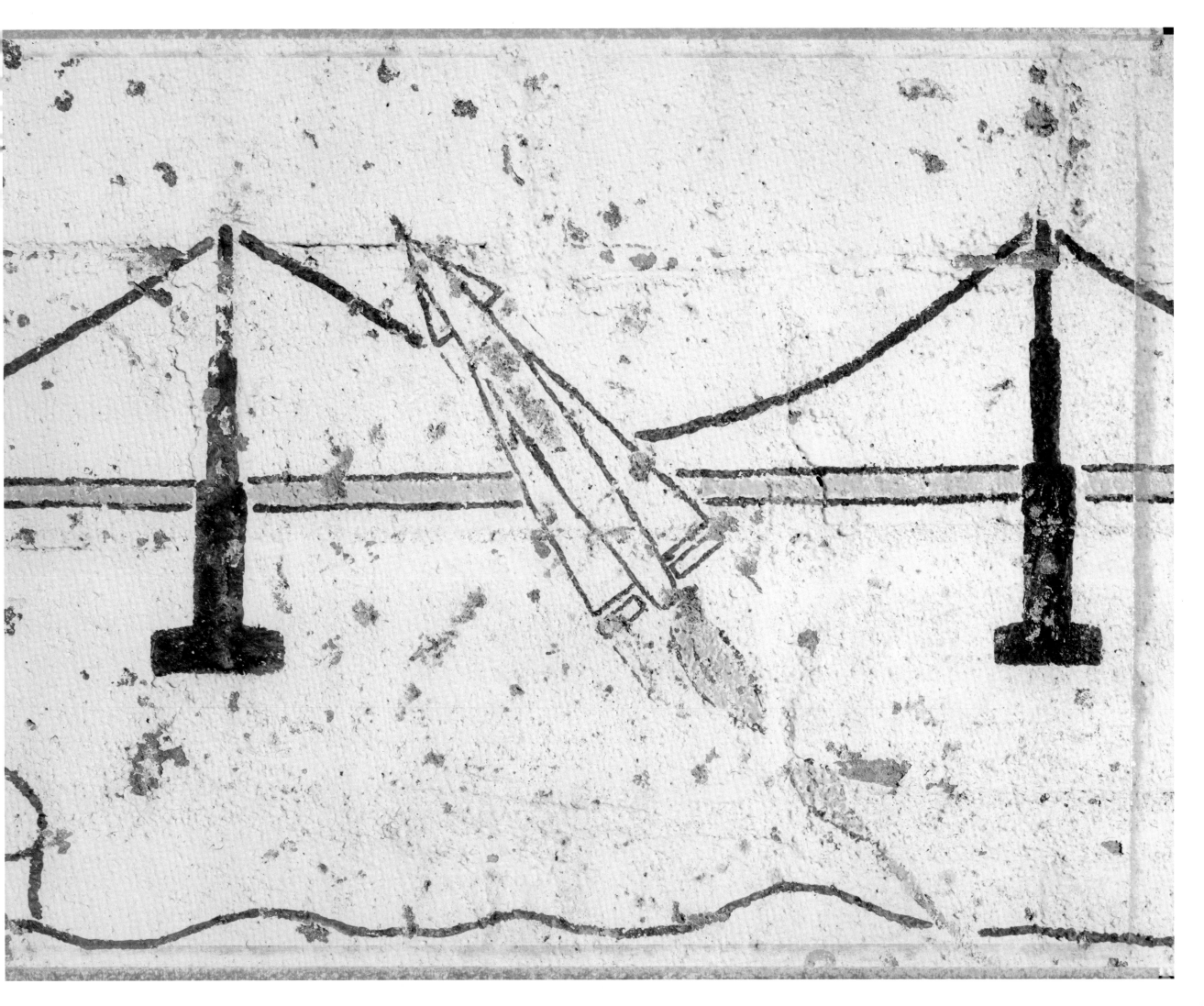

CHERYL KORALIK PICTURES OF PEACE

"I took these photographs of disabled people in small village communities in southern India, for Action on Disability and Development (ADD), in order to demonstrate what a positive contribution many disabled people make to their own communities. I came to understand that their real problem is the attitude of others.

"These people are at peace within the confines of their predicaments, a worthy lesson to us all...."

The Work Is Done, Chengham Village, 1990
Integration Through Fun, Chinnamustur Village, 1990
Independence—Sunkama Walking, Mopidi Village, 1990

ANNIE LEIBOVITZ PICTURES OF PEACE

"I was photographing dancers who were living and rehearsing during the summer at a wildlife refuge on the west coast of Florida. There was a feeling of so much freedom—a collision of spiritual and sexual energy.

"'If the world were at peace, what would you shoot?' It is hard to even imagine such a time. I just keep on working."

White Oak Project, Rob Berserer, 1990
White Oak Project, Florida, 1990
White Oak Project, Mark Morris, 1990

PETER LINDBERG PICTURES OF PEACE

"Everything on this planet seems to be about the forces of nature and
the forces of man.

"If the world were at peace what would I shoot? The same pictures."

The Force of Man, 1984–1990

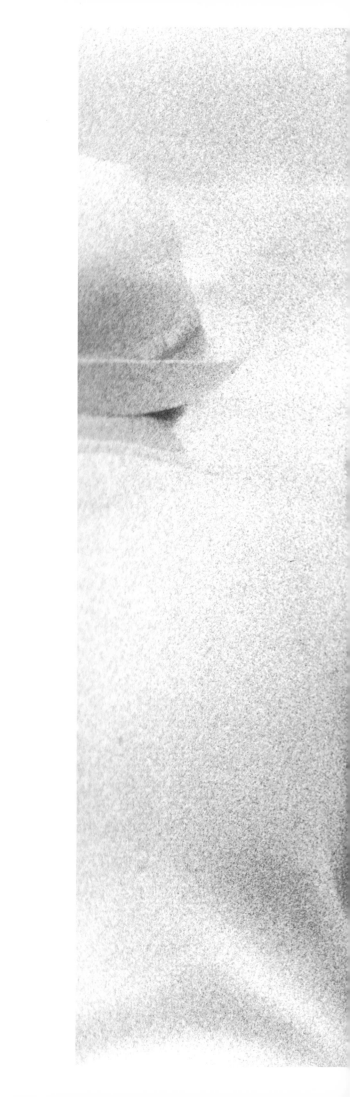

MARCIA LIPPMAN PICTURES OF PEACE

"These are my peace offerings. Images of harmony, friendship, tranquillity, and light."

Women on Wight, 1980
Mariel, Jessica, Adria, 1981
Ellis Island, 1989

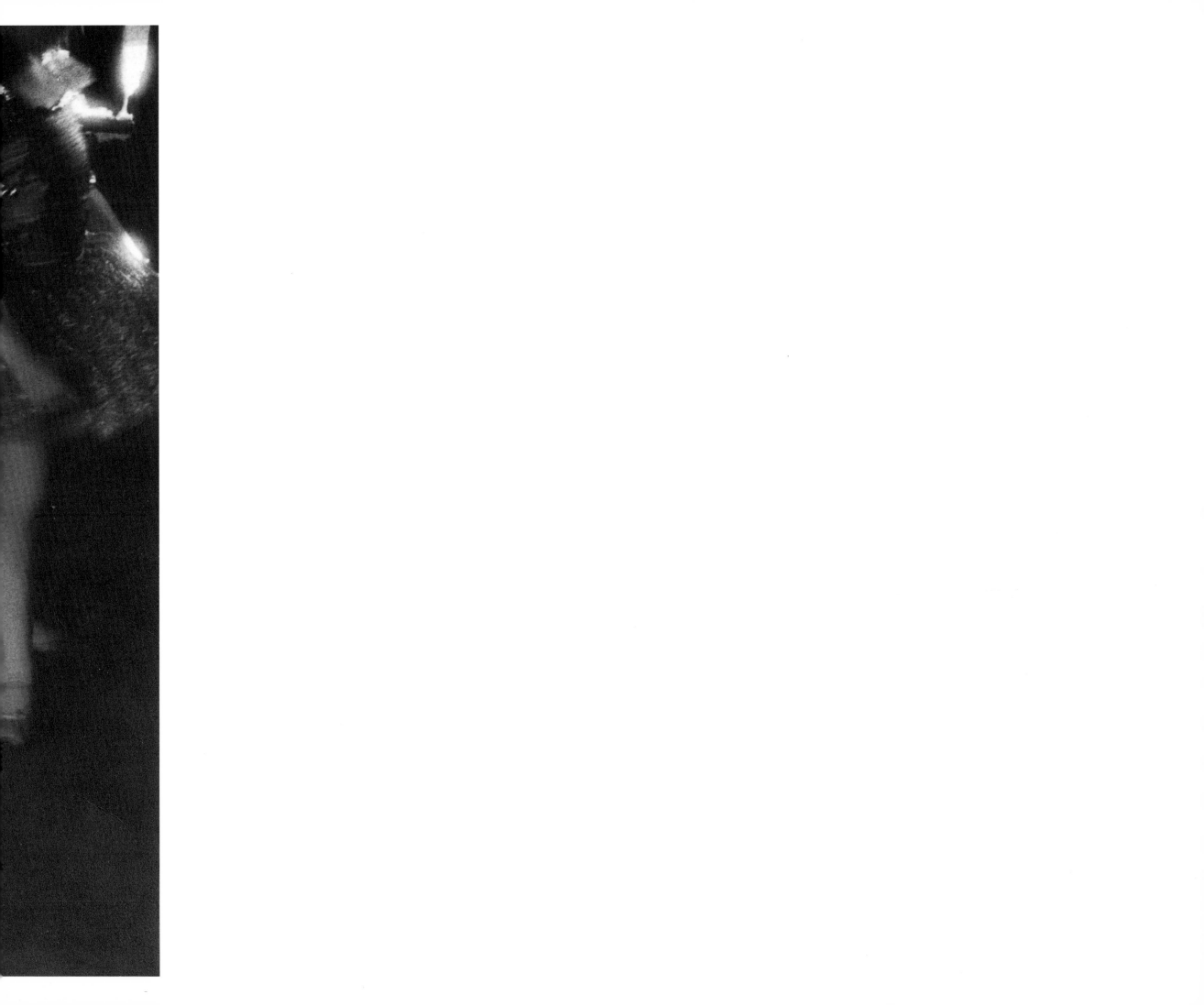

MARY ELLEN MARK PICTURES OF PEACE

"I chose these three images because they are recent and come from India, a country that I love. I feel they are powerful."

Wrestling School, Benares, 1989

School for the Blind, Benares, 1989

Young Girl Bathing in the Ganges River, 1989

KURT MARKUS PICTURES OF PEACE

"The pictures I like the most are the ones I have to explain the least.

"My hope for peace in the world is like a picture that works for more than just a moment...
one that can be around for a while, without tiring us, something that lasts."

Derrick Wince Y's for Living, Vicksburg, Mississippi, 1988
Greg Louganis, Hawaii, 1988

STEVEN MEISEL PICTURES OF PEACE

"Peace is a world without prejudice."

Pat Cleveland, New York, 1990

Wallace, Michelle, Josh, New York, 1989

SUSAN MEISELAS PICTURES OF PEACE

"It has been rare to share such moments in the midst of the conflicts I have
covered. 'If the world were at peace'...it seems to be impossible, nonetheless
worthy of our dreams."

Wedding, El Salvador, 1983

SHEILA METZNER PICTURES OF PEACE

"We can think of our children in terms of their future rather than
fear for their future."

Stella (Little Beach), upstate New York, 1989
One of a Kind, 1990

HERB RITTS PICTURES OF PEACE

"I chose this image because the Dalai Lama is an inspiration in the world.
The detail of his hand is praying for peace."

His Holiness the Dalai Lama, New York, 1987

PAOLO ROVERSI PICTURES OF PEACE

"There is no peace without love."

Kirsten in Paris, 1989
Jenny in London, 1987

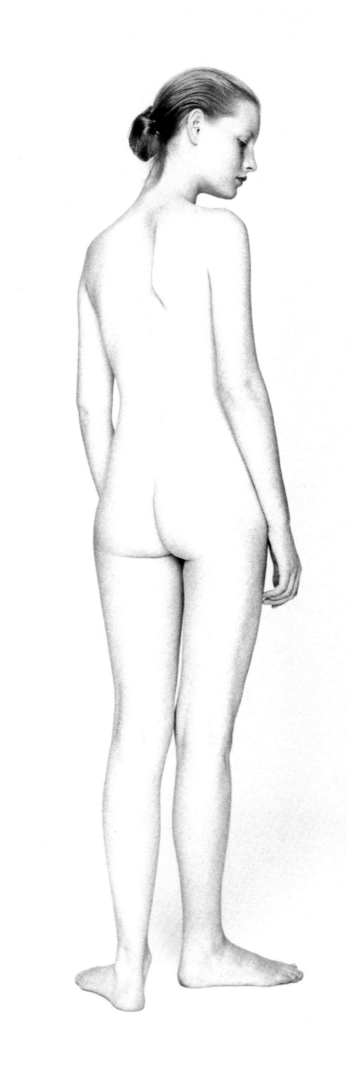

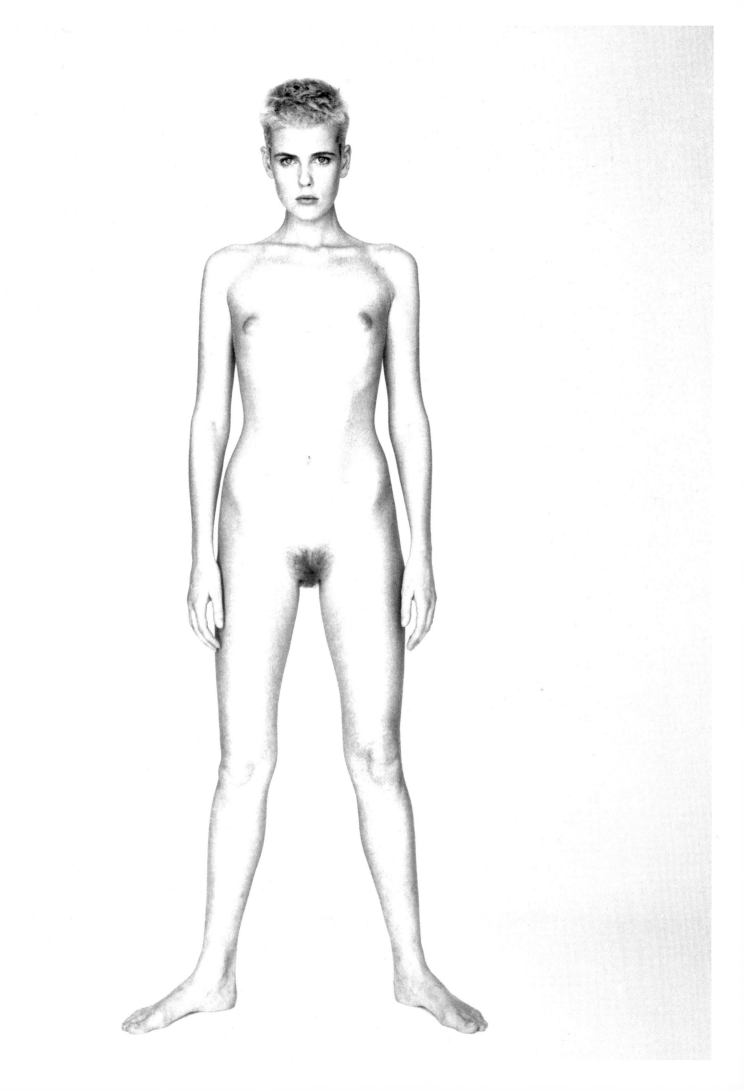

SEBASTIÃO SALGADO PICTURES OF PEACE

''We have the privilege to be part of an evolutionary process that leads us through
history. It is our responsibility as documentary photographers to show people
the social realities of our time.''

Ecuador, 1982
Ecuador, 1977
Ecuador, 1982

ALDO SESSA PICTURES OF PEACE

"I try to act with a hunter's stealth when I photograph people, in a way that I won't
 inhibit them. And, I try to shoot for the center of action—sometimes it's the eyes,
 sometimes the foot!

"Photography speaks, for me, a visceral language that comes from the soul. This
 feeling is close to what I imagine as peace."

Mataji Indra Devi, Rosedal, Buenos Aires, 1990
Pope John Paul II, foot, Teatro Colón, Buenos Aires, 1987
Pigeon, Academy of Fine Arts, Buenos Aires, 1988

BERT STERN PICTURES OF PEACE

"I try to photograph the spirit in people, which likens to peace, that which lies at the center of man's conflicts with life."

Marlon Brando, New York, 1959
Louis Armstrong, New York, 1955
Marilyn Monroe, Los Angeles, 1962

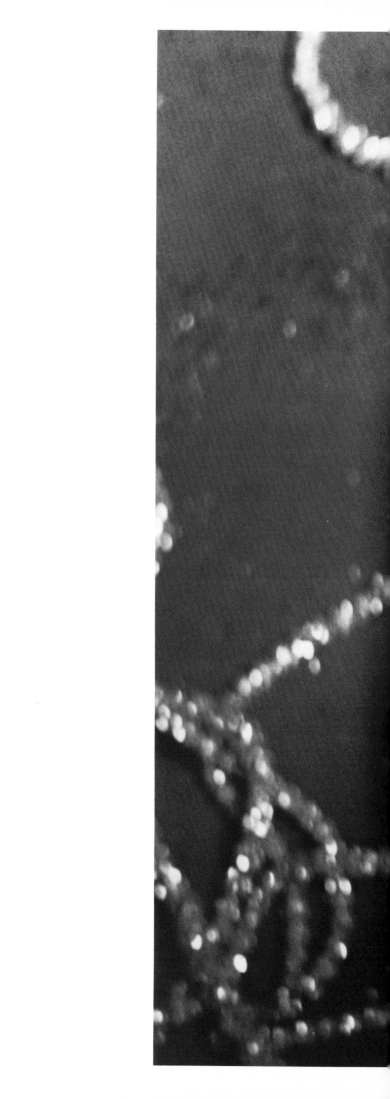

PHIL STERN PICTURES OF PEACE

"For over a half century, photography has been the means to earn my bread and my major joy as well. This 'job' has gotten me to traverse just about the entire globe and has given me the chance to rub elbows and break bread with some of God's most saintly and beautiful people as well as some of His most bastardly thugs.

"For all these decades I've been struggling, scratching, and clawing to make that one brilliantly definitive photograph which clearly explains humanity and the universe it inhabits.

"I, alas, have not been able to produce this image…yet."

Tru, 1962
Bogey and Steven, 1955
Louis Armstrong and Billie Holiday, New Orleans, 1949

JUDITH TURNER PICTURES OF PEACE

"Fragments of architecture, rather than overall views, allow for a new reading of form. Often a sense of harmony, order, and tranquility is evoked. This signifies, for me, a picture of peace."

The Cooper Union Renovation, John Hejduk, architect, New York, 1974
2 and 3, Private Residence, Robert Mallet-Stevens, architect, Paris, 1979

MAX VADUKUL   PICTURES OF PEACE

"If we want to enjoy the life of freedom, we have to take a stand against
those forces that threaten or deny us our human rights."

Water's Edge, Portofino, Italy, 1981
Beach, Long Island, New York, 1980
Old People, Coney Island, 1979

JAVIER VALLHONRAT PICTURES OF PEACE

"Through my work, I try to achieve a better comprehension of the meaning
of my reality. I look for the possibility of creating harmony between the specificity
of the photographic medium and my vision of the reality.

"I believe that photography allows me to deal simultaneously with the immediacy
of our existence and with the infinite, the eternal."

Animal—Vegetal, Madrid, December 1985
The Possessed Space, Circle, Madrid, November 1987

ALBERT WATSON PICTURES OF PEACE

Girl on a Beam, China, 1979

Baby Moccasins, New York, 1977

Man with Child, New York, 1987

"Lastly, she pictured to herself how this same little sister of hers would, in the after-time, be herself a grown woman; and how she would keep, through all her riper years, the simple and loving heart of her childhood; and how she would gather about her other little children, and make *their* eyes bright and eager with many a strange tale, perhaps even with the dream of Wonderland of long ago; and how she would feel with all their simple sorrows, and find a pleasure in all their simple joys, remembering her own child-life, and the happy summer days."

Lewis Carroll

"Love rears the great; Love tends the small;
Breaks off the yoke, breaks down the wall;
Accepteth all, fulfilleth all.

Sing hymns of Love, that those who hear
Far off in pain may lend an ear,
Rise up and wonder and draw near.

Lead lives of Love, that others who
Behold your lives may kindle too
With Love and cast their lots with you."

Christina Rossetti

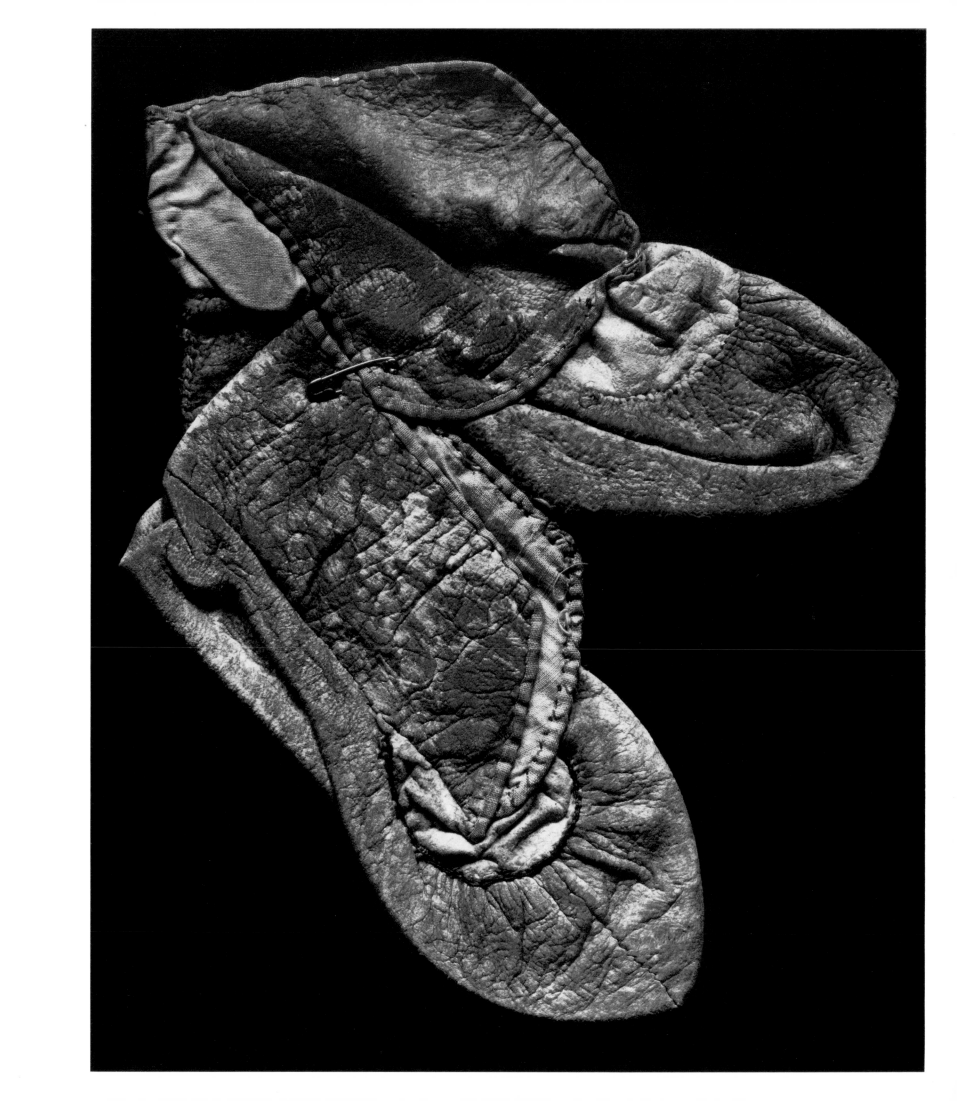

"For Mercy, Pity, Peace, and Love
  Is God, our father dear,
  And Mercy, Pity, Peace, and Love
  Is Man, his child and care.

For Mercy has a human heart,
  Pity a human face,
  And Love, the human form divine,
  And Peace, the human dress.

Then every man, of every clime,
  That prays in his distress,
  Prays to the human form divine,
  Love, Mercy, Pity, Peace."

                    William Blake

BRUCE WEBER PICTURES OF PEACE

"A day to remember: it was sunny along the Northern California coast and
everyone became a child again—filled with indulgences, spirit, and complete
abandonment, without any guilt.

"This is why I wanted to be part of this exhibition."

Lisa Marie in the Fields at Point Conception, California, 1988
Running at Point Conception, California, 1987
Running at Point Conception, California, 1987

ACKNOWLEDGMENTS

Thank you to all who have made this book and related events possible by devoting
your time, energy, and donations, and providing inspiration, up to the date of this
publication:

The photographers in this book, with special thanks to Bruce Weber and Peter Beard,
for their support, and Aldo Sessa for making the Buenos Aires show possible

Alberto Caputo

Lexington Labs

Sam Shahid

José de Paula Machado

Banco Boavista

Esprit

Grace Paley

Roland Algrant

Philip Feld

Conservation Framing Services

Vicky Wilson

Sid Rapoport

Matt Caputo

Mark Robertson

Juliette Galant

Fotofolio

Helene Condouris

Betty Eng

Hamilton Fish

Landey Strongin

Ester Kaufman

Aragão

Gavin Furlonger

Alexander Vreeland

Richard Martin

Rebecca Shafer

John Calcagno

Jean Jacque Naudet

Laura Steele

Sandy Seldin

Vicky Dwight

Didier Malige

Daniel Leser

Scott Berg

David Terry

Christian Steiner

Jerry and Gabriela Hirsch

Ursula Wöhlbier

Soloway and Levine